Historical Atlases of South Asia,
Central Asia, and the Middle East™

A HISTORICAL ATLAS OF

THE UNITED ARAB EMIRATES

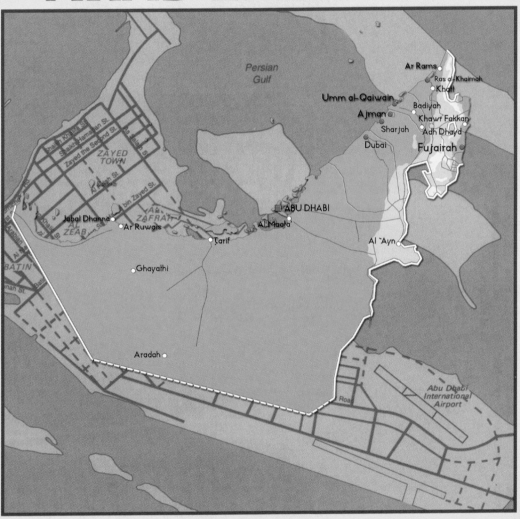

Amy Romano

The Rosen Publishing Group, Inc., New York

Thanks to those who provided an editorial eye along the way: Andrea, Rita, Jorge and Cathy, Carolyn and Steve.

Published in 2004 by The Rosen Publishing Group, Inc.
29 East 21st Street, New York, NY 10010

First Edition

Library of Congress Cataloging-in-Publication Data
Romano, Amy.
A historical atlas of the United Arab Emirates/Amy Romano.—1st ed.
    p. cm.—(Historical atlases of South Asia, Central Asia, and the Middle East)
Summary: Maps and text chronicle the history of the United Arab Emirates, a federation of seven independent sheikhdoms situated on the Arabian peninsula. Includes bibliographical references and index.
Contents: Antiquity in Arabia—Greeks, Persians, and the coming of Islam—European influence—The British—The era of oil—Independence—The modern UAE.
ISBN 0-8239-4501-4 (lib. bdg.)
1. United Arab Emirates—History—Maps for children. 2. United Arab Emirates—Maps for children. [1. United Arab Emirates—History. 2. Atlases]
I. Title. II. Series.

G2249.76.S1R6 2004
911'.5357—dc22

                                                                          2003055017

Manufactured in the United States of America

On the cover: The president of the United Arab Emirates, Sheikh Zayed bin Sultan al-Nahyan (bottom left), the Grand Mosque in Dubai (bottom right), and an eighteenth-century Islamic painting (top) are shown in front of a contemporary map of the United Arab Emirates (foreground) and a city map of Abu Dhabi (background).

Contents

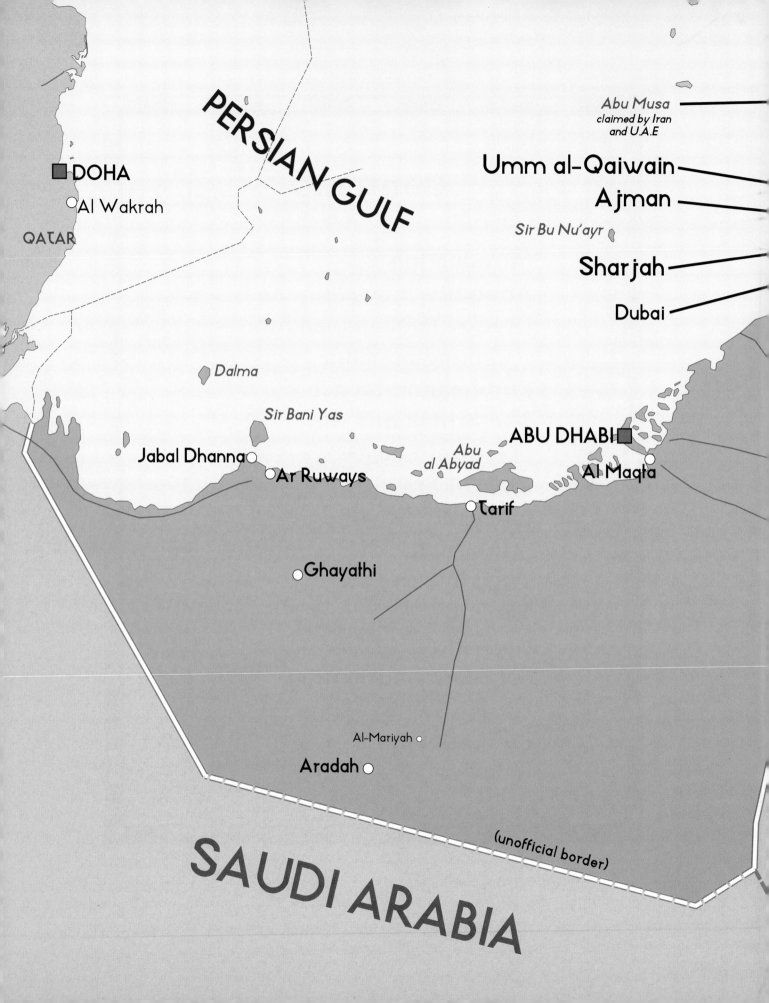

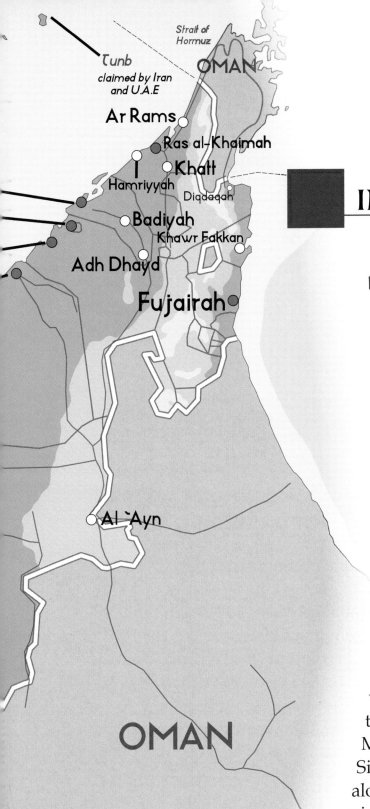

Strait of Hormuz

OMAN

Tunb
claimed by Iran
and U.A.E

Ar Rams

Ras al-Khaimah

Khatt

Hamriyyah

Diqdaqah

Badiyah

Khawr Fakkan

Adh Dhayd

Fujairah

Al `Ayn

OMAN

INTRODUCTION

The United Arab Emirates (UAE) is a federation of seven independent Arab sheikhdoms. The UAE is located in the southeastern corner of the Arabian Peninsula. A sheikhdom is a territory ruled by an Islamic religious leader called an emir. An infant country compared to the long history of the region, the UAE did not gain independence until 1971. Since then, events and alliances within the UAE have had a tremendous impact on the entire world.

Although the Arabian Peninsula is rich in history, establishing early records for the UAE has been difficult. Little archaeological research took place there prior to the nation's independence. Despite this lack of information, it is widely accepted that humans populated the foothills of the northeastern Hajar Mountains between 6000 and 5000 BC. Significant archaeological discoveries along the Persian Gulf coast also indicate widespread ancient civilizations composed

This contemporary map of the United Arab Emirates shows its position on the Arabian Peninsula. The UAE is bordered by Qatar, the Persian Gulf, Saudi Arabia (with a boundary that was formalized in the 1990s but not made public), and Oman (with a boundary that was finalized in 2003). Although the UAE gained its independence from Great Britain in 1971, Iran and Saudi Arabia have both contended that sections of the UAE are theirs according to historic tribal claims. Today, people living in the UAE maintain a high standard of living as a result of the enormous export of petroleum.

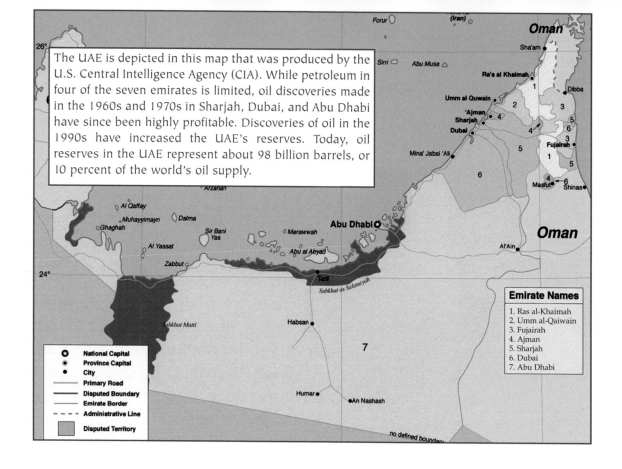

The UAE is depicted in this map that was produced by the U.S. Central Intelligence Agency (CIA). While petroleum in four of the seven emirates is limited, oil discoveries made in the 1960s and 1970s in Sharjah, Dubai, and Abu Dhabi have since been highly profitable. Discoveries of oil in the 1990s have increased the UAE's reserves. Today, oil reserves in the UAE represent about 98 billion barrels, or 10 percent of the world's oil supply.

Emirate Names

1. Ras al-Khaimah
2. Umm al-Qaiwain
3. Fujairah
4. Ajman
5. Sharjah
6. Dubai
7. Abu Dhabi

of fishermen, tradesmen, and farmers. These early civilizations were prosperous. Unfortunately, this prosperity was short-lived. The region later spent centuries as one of the poorest areas in the world.

A crescent-shaped country covering approximately 32,380 square miles (83,864 square kilometers), the UAE is roughly the size of the state of Maine. It shares land borders with Qatar in the northwest, Oman in the east, and Saudi Arabia in the west and south. The Saudi border is the UAE's longest continuous land border, running primarily through desert. This boundary is undisclosed. For years, it has been a border of con-

tention between the emirates, as well as the topic of ongoing debates with the Saudi Arabian government. The UAE's northern boundary is an 819-mile (1,318 km) stretch of coastline shared between the Persian Gulf and the Gulf of Oman.

In the early twentieth century, the discovery of oil and gas deposits in the UAE set the stage for a remarkable transformation in the region. It would not be long before the modern UAE—Abu Dhabi, Dubai, Sharjah, Ajman, Umm al-Qaiwain, Ras al-Khaimah, and Fujairah—rose out of poverty to unite and become one of the world's wealthiest nations.

1 ANTIQUITY IN ARABIA

The ancient history of the United Arab Emirates is found largely in the evolution of Arabia. The Arabian Peninsula is a desert peninsula in the extreme southwestern section of Asia with a total area of about 1.2 million square miles (3.1 million sq. km). This area is home to the modern countries of Saudi Arabia, Yemen, Oman, Qatar, Kuwait, Bahrain, and the United Arab Emirates.

Early Inhabitants

Inhabited by countless tribal units, the early history of Arabia is a kaleidoscope of changing relationships. While it is not known exactly when tribes first settled the region, archaeological evidence indicates that sophisticated cultures existed around Jebel Hafit some 6,000 years ago. This area is often referred to as the Buraimi Oasis. Archaeological findings, which include tombs and evidence that crops like wheat, dates, and barley were cultivated, date to the third and fourth millennia BC. In order for these crops to have survived, the desert climate had to have been much cooler than it is today. Evidence also reveals that the inhabitants of this region were a Semitic-speaking people. They migrated into the Tigris and Euphrates River valleys

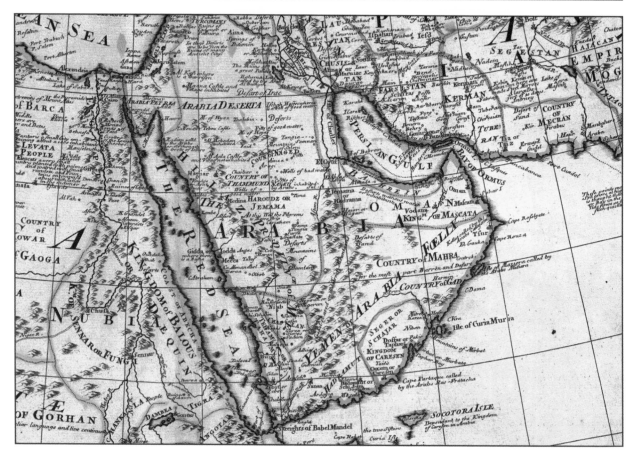

This map of the Arabian Peninsula was designed by John Senex, an eighteenth-century British cartographer under Queen Anne. The map was first printed in *A New General Atlas* in 1721. At the time, Arabia was commonly known by its Latin name, Arabia Felix, which translates to "happy land to the right of Mecca," the Muslim holy city. The area that would later become the UAE is labeled on this map as Oman.

in Mesopotamia (present-day Iraq and eastern Syria) around 3500 BC. These Semitic people spoke a Semitic language such as Arabic or Hebrew. This particular group came to be known as the Assyro-Babylonians. Future civilizations, such as the Ammorites and Canaanites, also of Arabian descent, migrated out of Arabia to the Mediterranean Sea beginning around 2500 BC.

An important influence in the region was an early empire called Magan. The Magans were an independent power. They were once part of the Akkadian Empire based near Sumer, in Mesopotamia. The Magan Empire ruled Arabia from the region that makes up Oman and the UAE today. The empire attained its considerable wealth from mining copper deposits found in the hills around Suhar, Oman.

Archaeological findings on the northeastern outskirts of Dubai suggest that the Magan Empire also maintained communities in the UAE. These settlements stretched at least as far as the Persian Gulf. Burial tombs, referred to as Hafit, named because of the location of their discovery, and beehive tombs, named after their honeycomblike shape, link these locations. Archaeological dating and similar construction styles and artifacts provide evidence that these separate civilizations were possibly unified in a single culture.

Umm an-Nar

Between 2500 and 2000 BC, at the beginning of the Bronze Age, a new and distinct culture appeared around Abu Dhabi. This culture was called Umm an-Nar (also Umm al-Nar). Its inhabitants are presumed to have been artisans and fishermen. They were also one of the first civilizations to domesticate the camel, an animal significant to Arabia.

The Umm an-Nar civilization was very influential in the development of Arab culture, although it thrived for only a few centuries. During this time, pottery and other crafts flourished. Discoveries of

Created between 2100 and 2000 BC, this model of a plowing scene thought to have originated with the Umm an-Nar ("Mother of Fire") civilization.

pottery, beads, and daggers indicate the Umm an-Nar was likely linked through trade with civilizations of the Indus Valley in present-day Pakistan and Afghanistan.

This evidence, and that of additional settlements discovered at Badiyah (in Fujairah) and Rams (near Ras al-Khaimah), date to the third millennium BC. It is believed that these and most other cities of ancient Arabia derived their wealth from their position on trade routes between Mesopotamia and the Indus Valley. In addition to traditional Bedouin activities such as herding and farming, countries of the gulf became centers of shipping and shipbuilding.

The Iron Age

Three distinct kingdoms had emerged in Arabia by 1000 BC, beginning a 1,700-year period of unification in the region.

The Minaeans were the first of these Semitic kingdoms to develop. The Minaeans are believed to have existed from 1200 to 650 BC. They administered the activities of their

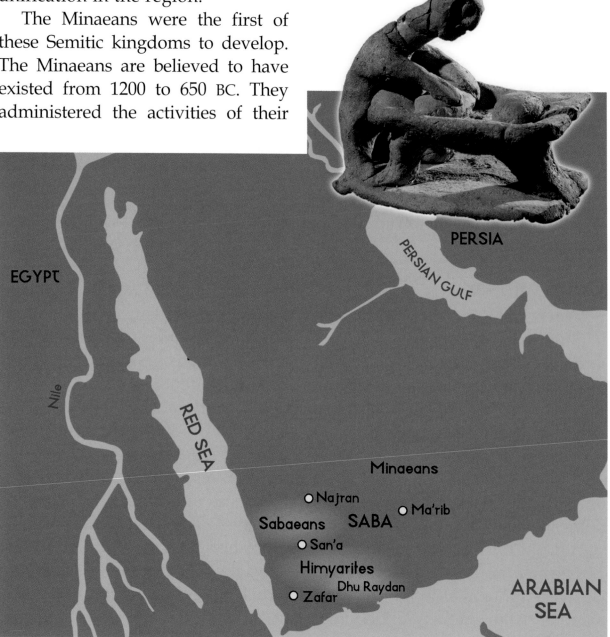

The most prominent kingdoms of the Iron Age and the approximate locations of their settlements are pictured on this map of Arabia. Trade flourished between the Minaeans, the Sabaeans, and the Himyarites. These cultures likely traded with the Phoenicians. The Phoenicians were the ancient master mariners of the Levant (present-day countries such as Syria, Lebanon, and Israel) who were widely traveled and may have even circumnavigated the African continent. This Phoenician clay artifact (*inset*) from the same period depicts a baker.

kingdom from the Southern Arabian interior in what is now Yemen. Eventually, they populated the entire Arabian Peninsula. The Minaeans were a peaceful community of traders. Their government maintained features of a democracy and the formation of a city-state. The Minaean capital, Ma'in, and eventually its empire fell to the Sabaeans late in the second century BC.

The Sabaean kingdom was founded around 930 BC and flourished until about 115 BC. Sabaean leaders ruled from a region that is commonly referred to as Saba' (or Sheba) in southwestern Arabia. It has been suggested that the Queen of Sheba mentioned in the Bible as having visited King Solomon in Jerusalem was Sabaean. When the Sabaeans defeated the Minaeans,

This Arab man cuts into a Frankincense tree to collect its valuable gum resin. Incisions made into the tree immediately produce a milky sap, which, when air-dried, will turn into resin. It is this dried resin that is commonly burned to produce an aromatic fragrance. Frankincense, a valuable commodity during ancient times, was used by the Egyptians for embalming and in cosmetics such as eyeliner. It was also used by the Greeks and Romans for ceremonial purposes and by the Arabs as medicine.

they assumed control only of the existing Minaean territory. The Sabaeans failed in their attempts to unify and expand the region.

The third in this line of southern Arabian rulers was the Himyarites. The Himyarites ruled the region from 115 BC to AD 525 until the kingdom fell under Abyssinian control. During the Himyarite reign, Arabia prospered by trading frankincense, myrrh, and spices such as pepper, cloves, cinnamon, and ginger. Frankincense and myrrh are aromatic gum resins commonly used in the production of perfume and incense. The prosperity of the southern lands was mirrored in the north (present-day UAE and Oman) through pearl diving and other sea-based economies.

Innovation

While Semitic leadership was changing hands in the south, two significant events were occurring in the northern region. The first was the domestication of the camel, believed to have occurred between 1200 and 300 BC. Camel caravans revolutionized land transportation in the desert and accelerated the development of overland trade routes.

Camels

The camel is primarily a desert animal that can travel great distances with little food and water. Its endurance and strength have made it a valuable beast of burden, instrumental in the development of many ancient civilizations. There are two kinds of camels—the Arabian camel, also called the dromedary, and the Bactrian camel. Dromedary camels are characterized by a single hump; Bactrian camels have two humps. The humps are essentially stores of flesh and fat, absorbed as nutrition when food is scarce.

Arabs domesticated camels between 6,000 and 4,000 years ago to promote caravan trading. Bedouin, or desert nomads, commonly drink camel's milk; use camel hair and hides for tents, blankets, rugs, and clothing; and even burn camel dung as fuel. Camels are also used for sport. These camels in the UAE are being cared for prior to a race.

A traditional *aflaj* channel irrigation system can be seen surrounding this man in Oman. Each channel where water flows down from the mountains is called a *falaj*. In order to utilize the water more efficiently, crops are normally grown at varied heights so that water runoff from one tier can irrigate plantings on a lower tier.

The second dramatic innovation was the development of *falaj* irrigation, a technique that uses underground channels to bring water from the mountains to the desert. *Aflaj* systems greatly improved the region's ability to cultivate crops in a harsh desert environment. Some of these ancient channels are still in use today in the Buraimi Oasis area on UAE's eastern border.

2 GREEKS, PERSIANS, AND THE COMING OF ISLAM

As the first century AD approached, several tribal dynasties existed in Arabia. Each of these dynasties would have a profound influence in the development of Arab cultural and religious identities. During the Middle Ages (350–1450), the United Arab Emirates was incorporated into the kingdom of Hormuz, based on the island of Hormuz. The island of Hormuz is located in the strait of Hormuz that links the Persian Gulf and the Arabian Sea (or Gulf of Oman).

In southern Arabia, the authority of the Minaean, Sabaean, and Himyarite dynasties was stable, except for brief invasions. Conflicts during this period erupted with Aksumite kings from Ethiopia in 525 and 300 BC and the Greeks in 24 BC. A complete conquest of Arabia never occurred at this time. The vast deserts of the peninsula presented too great an obstacle for early civilizations. As a result, southern powers

The extent of the Nabataean kingdom and its capital city of Petra may be seen in this map that depicts the Arabian Peninsula between the first centuries BC and AD. Made wealthy and successful due to their monopoly on Arabia's caravan trade, the Nabataeans were an advanced culture that was responsible for developing the Arabic that would be used to record Muhammad's revelations in writing. The Nabataeans were allies of the Romans, whose influence can still be seen in Petra's architectural ruins today.

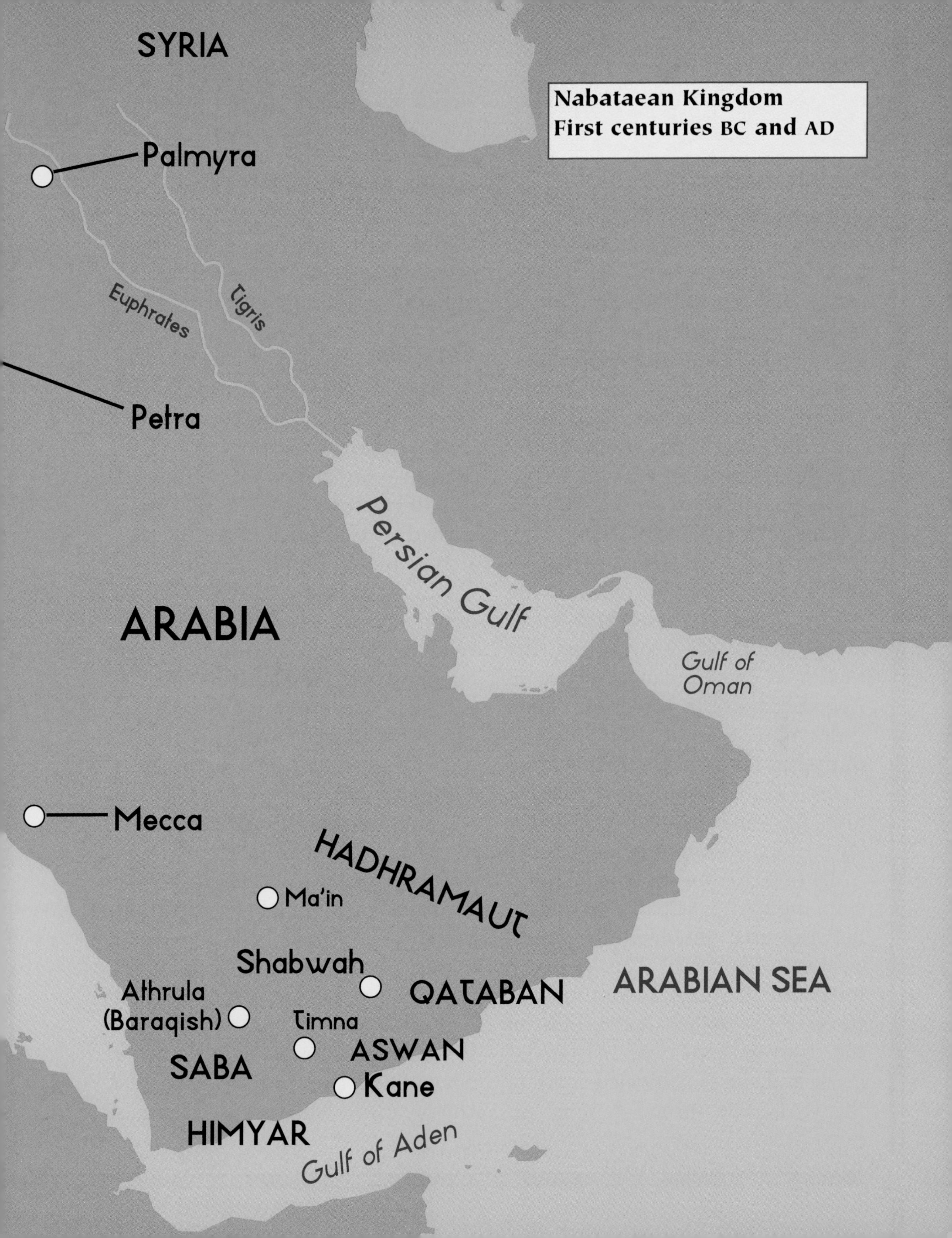

SYRIA

Palmyra

Euphrates

Tigris

Petra

Persian Gulf

Gulf of Oman

**Nabataean Kingdom
First centuries BC and AD**

ARABIA

Mecca

HADHRAMAUT

Ma'in

ARABIAN SEA

Shabwah

Athrula
(Baraqish)

QATABAN

Timna

ASWAN

SABA

Kane

HIMYAR

Gulf of Aden

remained separate from the ruling houses of the north.

Nabataeans to Greeks

The earliest of the northern ruling houses were the Nabataeans. The Nabataean kingdom, which briefly extended from Arabia as far north as Damascus in present-day Syria, greatly influenced cultural and religious developments in Arabia. Ruling from their capital in Petra (now in present-day Jordan), the Nabataeans are credited with developing the Arabic script used in the Koran, the holy book of Islam.

Through an advance ordered by the Roman general Trajan, Rome gained control of the Nabataean kingdom in AD 106, ruling the region as the Roman province of Arabia Petraea. In power for only a little more than a century, their impact in the region is still evident today. Ruins found near Sharjah and in Umm al-Qaiwain show strong Greco-Roman influences.

During the time of Roman leadership, the UAE was part of a trading network that involved the entire Arabian Peninsula. This network linked Mediterranean countries with those of the Indian Ocean. Most of the caravan trade was in frankincense and spices cultivated south of the UAE. The second century AD would also see a boom in maritime trade that involved the entire gulf region. This evolution prompted the interest of numerous foreign powers. Soon, much of the Arabian Peninsula would be viewed as a valuable property to be dominated rather than developed.

Persians

As trade through Arabia flourished, Persian forces that had been present in the region as far back as 563 BC exerted more control in Arabia. At this time, portions of the UAE existed as territories of the Persian Achaemenid Empire. Later, the Sassanid dynasty, also of Persia, dominated the area. The Sassanids actively attempted to control the booming sea-based trade in the gulf.

The Sassanids occupied the region for about 400 years, establishing inland settlements as well as communities along the coast. Sassanid rule was brought to an end by Islamic tribes from the Arabian interior, namely the Umayyads. The Umayyads destroyed the Sassanids presence in Arabia. The Umayyad dynasty became the first great Muslim empire to rule a unified Arab kingdom. This advance of Islam unified Arabia in religion, if not politics. During their reign, the Umayyads established settlements

This seventeenth-century Persian miniature depicts a Sassanid prince. The Sassanid dynasty was a medieval empire that lasted about 400 years beginning in AD 224. At its height, Sassanid territories extended west from present-day Afghanistan through Iran and Iraq.

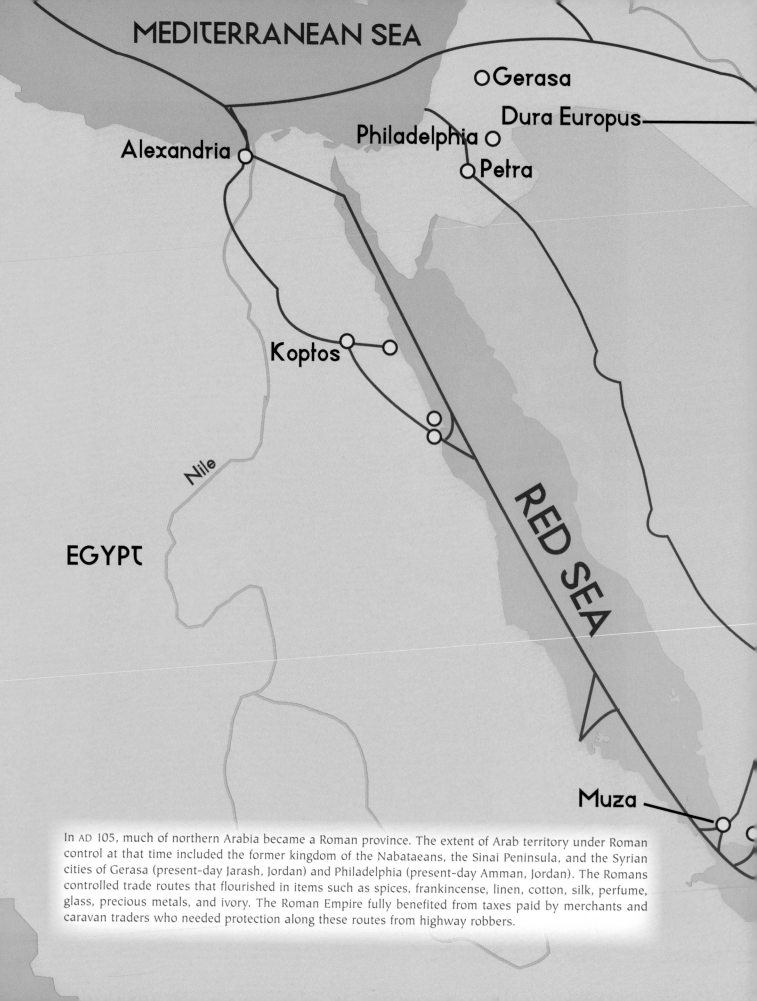

MEDITERRANEAN SEA

○Gerasa

Dura Europus

Philadelphia ○

○Petra

Alexandria ○

Koptos ○

Nile

EGYPT

RED SEA

Muza

In AD 105, much of northern Arabia became a Roman province. The extent of Arab territory under Roman control at that time included the former kingdom of the Nabataeans, the Sinai Peninsula, and the Syrian cities of Gerasa (present-day Jarash, Jordan) and Philadelphia (present-day Amman, Jordan). The Romans controlled trade routes that flourished in items such as spices, frankincense, linen, cotton, silk, perfume, glass, precious metals, and ivory. The Roman Empire fully benefited from taxes paid by merchants and caravan traders who needed protection along these routes from highway robbers.

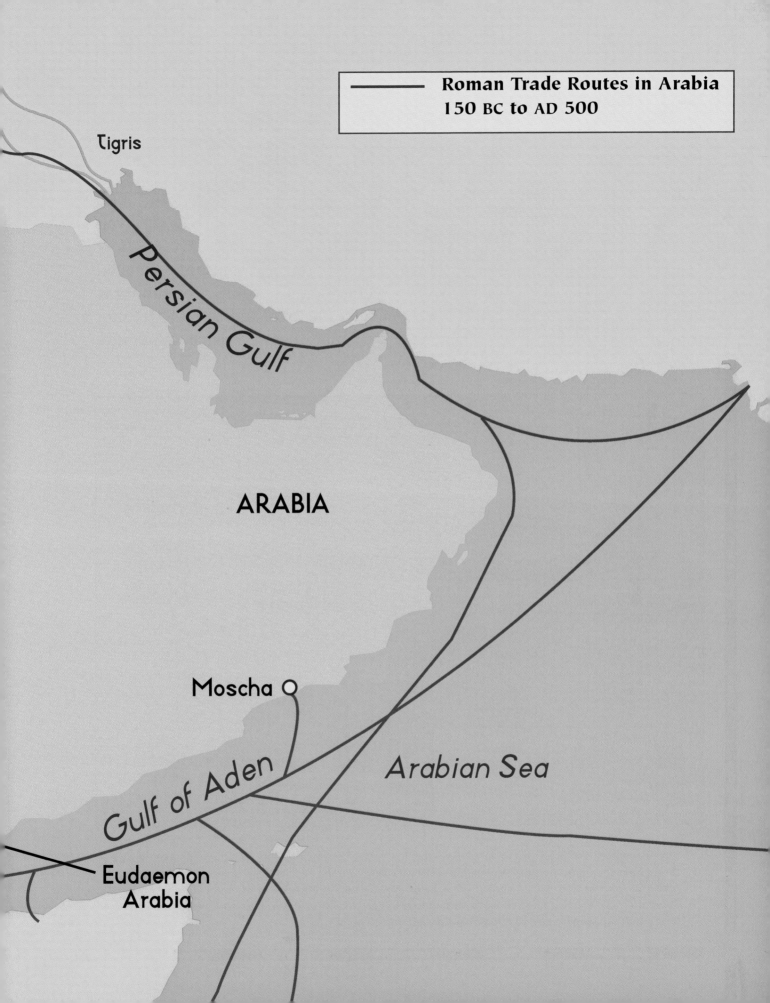

Tigris

Persian Gulf

ARABIA

Moscha O

Gulf of Aden

Arabian Sea

Eudaemon
Arabia

in what is now the emirate of Ras al-Khaimah, and at Al-Qusais and Jumeria in present-day Dubai.

The Emergence of Islam

With the Umayyad dynasty firmly in control, Arab migration increased. Between AD 200 and 600, Arab tribes from the south and east (primarily Yemen and areas of Saudi Arabia) entered the region. These new communities built economies based on farming, fishing, trading, and nomadic grazing. They governed themselves though the Arab system of consultation and agreement known as "desert democracy."

The incoming Arab tribes found the inland oases and wadis (dry valleys through which rivers flow during the rainy season) inhabited with Persian farming communities. Unlike the tribal and nomadic traits of the Arabs, these Persian communities

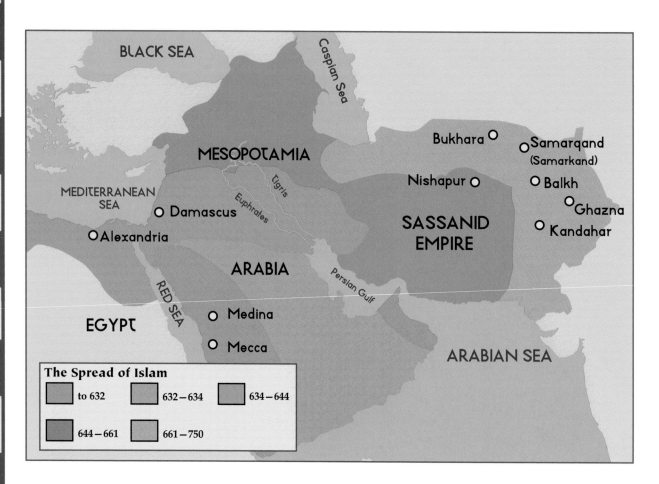

The emergence of Islam began in Mecca, the birthplace of the prophet Muhammad, and advanced throughout the entire Arabian Peninsula. Islam was able to unite rival tribes under one god (Allah), and powerful Arab armies helped spread the religion rapidly within decades of Muhammad's death in 632. Soon after, Islam had gained converts throughout the Levant. By 650, the Persian Empire had embraced Islam, and the religion gained a foothold throughout the Middle East.

were centralized. At first, differences led to fighting between Persians and Arabs. Eventually, however, Arabia's new Arab inhabitants established separate communities and created independent societies. Along with their culture and governing style, the Arabs brought with them the power of a new religion known as Islam, a word meaning "submission."

The followers of Islam, which is based on the teachings of the prophet Muhammad, are known as Muslims. The majority of Muslims who inhabited the area were orthodox Sunnis. Sunni Muslims do not make distinctions between religion, morality, and legal affairs. They believe that all aspects of their public and private lives are dictated in the words of the Koran. Today, the majority of the world's Muslim population is Sunni.

According to the Koran, Muhammad was born in Mecca in western Arabia. He received his first revelation in AD 610 and began preaching these revelations

Islam

Islam is the name given to the religion preached by the prophet Muhammad, beginning in AD 613. It is the world's second largest religion after Christianity. There are three historic divisions all built on the central concept of *tawhid*, or the oneness of God. Regardless of sect or division, however, a person who follows Islam is called a Muslim.

The majority of Muslims belong to the Sunni sect. Most conservative Muslims are Sunnis who follow a strict approach to religion. Sunni Muslims reject modern and popular interpretation of Islamic law. The next largest sect is the Shia, whose members are called Shiites. Among the Shiites, the Imami are the largest group. Finally, the smallest sect of Islamic followers is the Kharijites. These Muslims believe in a precise interpretation of the Koran and are renowned for their belief in total equality under God, whom Muslims call Allah.

Revelations that would later make up the Koran are revealed to the prophet Muhammad during a battle in this eighteenth-century Islamic painting.

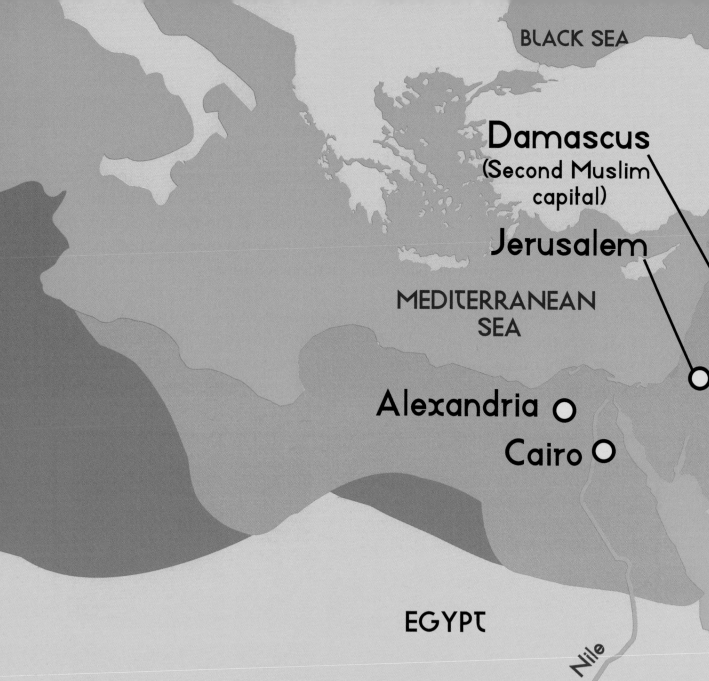

BLACK SEA

Damascus
(Second Muslim
capital)

Jerusalem

MEDITERRANEAN
SEA

Alexandria O

Cairo O

EGYPT

Nile

Muslim Empire, Umayyad Caliphate (AD 661–750)

AD 632, after the death of Muhammad

AD 656, after the death of Uthman

AD 660, after the death of Ali

⭑ Capital city

The expanse of the Muslim Empire is portrayed in this map that shows its various capital cities between AD 661 and 750, a period dominated by the Umayyad dynasty. This map illustrates the dynasty under various caliphs and shows changes in the Muslim capital from Medina to Damascus and, later, to Baghdad.

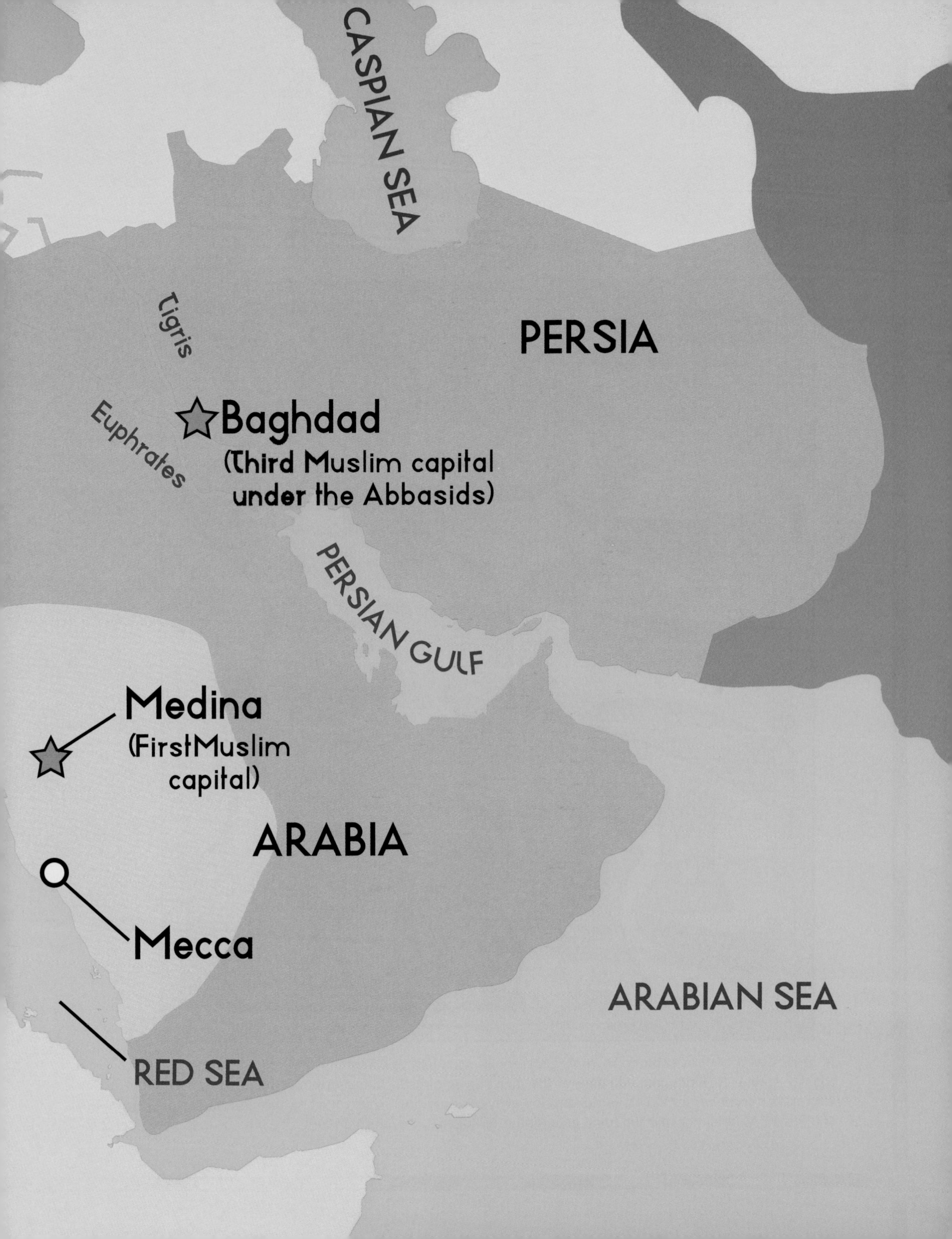

CASPIAN SEA

Tigris

Euphrates

PERSIA

☆ Baghdad
(Third Muslim capital
under the Abbasids)

PERSIAN GULF

Medina
(First Muslim
capital)

ARABIA

Mecca

RED SEA

ARABIAN SEA

three years later. He continued to do so until his death in 632. In 635, a Muslim dynasty victory over the Umayyads occurred at Dibba, a port city located at the border between the UAE and Oman. Dibba was an export center of the copper industry in pre-Islamic Arabia. It is noted for being the last Arabian stronghold against the spread of Islam throughout the region.

Al Idrisi was a twelfth-century AD Arab geographer, scientist, and writer who created this 1182 map of coastal Arabia. Al Idrisi created some of the major geographical manuscripts of his lifetime, combining information from earlier Greek works and his own observations. After traveling throughout North Africa and Spain, Al Idrisi became the royal geographer of Roger II, the Norman king of Sicily, in 1145.

This Muslim victory traditionally marks the completion of the Islamic conquest of the Arabian Peninsula. Within a century, Muslim armies had conquered an enormous empire stretching from Spain to India.

Changes

The advance of Islam throughout Arabia marked the end of one era and the beginning of another. It also indicates the point in time in which the histories of the seven Arabian countries diverge.

Within thirty years of Muhammad's death, Muslim rulers relocated the capital of the Muslim Empire from Medina to Damascus. With this move, Arabia became an increasingly less important world player. Previous periods of prosperity and of political and religious authority were over. In 751, another shift of the Islamic center from Damascus to Baghdad led to further decline.

From this point through much of the tenth century, the land later known as the UAE became a Muslim province under the caliphs of the Abbasid dynasty. However, Arabia did unify briefly under an Islamic sect known as the Karmathians during the tenth century. Afterward, local tribes would again disunite.

External interest in the gulf would not rise again until the fifteenth century. By this time, foreign interests tried to create the appearance of a unified and prosperous Arabia. Ultimately, the taste of economic growth would encourage these countries to compete for political independence.

3 EUROPEAN INFLUENCE

Portugal was the first European power to take an active interest in the Persian Gulf. Portuguese explorer Vasco da Gama made the first known reference to this area in 1498 when he traveled through the Strait of Hormuz to the sheikhdom of Julfar. This area is now a part of the United Arab Emirates. In 1507, another Portuguese navigator named Alfonso de Albuquerque captured the island of Hormuz at the entrance of the gulf. In less than two decades, Portuguese forces occupied Julfar and controlled the lower gulf region. Eventually, the Portuguese extended their presence as far north as the island nation of Bahrain.

The Portuguese had intended to build an empire in India. To do so they believed they needed to control the sea routes linking Lisbon, Portugal, to Bombay (Mumbai) and Goa in India,

The routes of various European explorers to the Americas, Africa, India, and Asia are illustrated in this map that details navigational achievements during the European age of discovery between 1340 and 1600. More important, this map details the routes of Vasco da Gama and Alfonso de Albuquerque, who helped Portugal gain trading access to Arabia and India. As a result of their explorations, the Portuguese gained control of trading in the gulf and amassed huge fortunes.

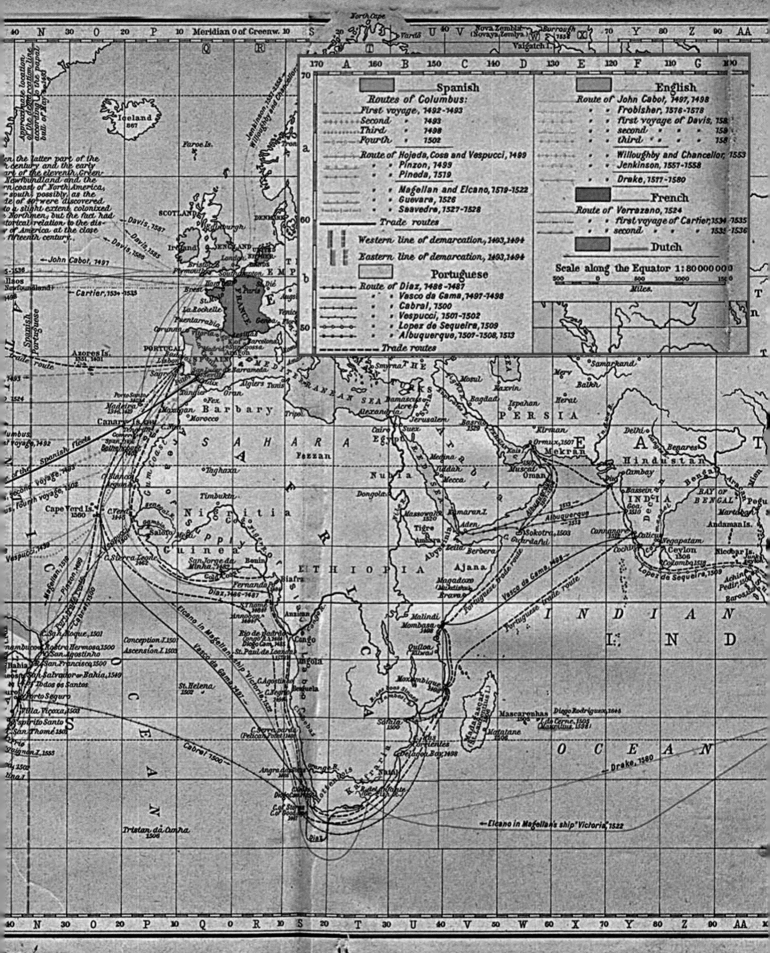

This seventeenth-century Persian manuscript depicts a sea battle between Arab and Portuguese forces in the Strait of Hormuz. The Portuguese captured the island and Strait of Hormuz in the Persian Gulf, along with the city of Julfar (present-day Ras al-Khaimah), thus securing their control over gulf trade for nearly a century.

namely the Persian Gulf and the Strait of Hormuz. While in Julfar, Portuguese traders built custom-houses. They amassed great fortunes from taxing and controlling the goods through these waterways.

The British

Portuguese control in the gulf continued for just over a century. In 1633, a sea-based invasion of Dutch and British forces of the East India Company began. This emergence of the British, combined with land attacks of local tribes, forced the Portuguese to retreat.

By 1600, India had become a profitable colony for Great Britain, and the Portuguese presence in the gulf interfered with the ambitions of British traders. At the time, the Portuguese controlled shipping, imposed heavy taxes, and treated people badly. They often imprisoned and tortured those who opposed them. In order for Great Britain to preserve its access to gulf shipping lanes and to maintain India's profitability, it had to act.

With the 1633 advance of the East India Company forces, the British dominated Portuguese sailors. Soon the British became the most dominant foreign power in the region. Initially, their interest was not in the developments of the emirates, but in their own profits. As a result, political control changed. It passed first to the powerful tribes of Oman. Then control over the gulf was passed briefly to the Persians before local tribes took control of the land for themselves.

The Qawasim and the Bani Yas

The British influence increased in the gulf during the eighteenth century. These changes, along with the development of various political

Pearling

The pearling industry helped transform the traditional economy of the emirates' tribal population. Many families who had started pearling to supplement farming and herding activities moved to permanent coastal settlements. This migration was instrumental in increasing both the size and importance of Abu Dhabi and Dubai. The other coastal sheikhdoms of Sharjah and Ras al-Khaimah (formerly Julfar) and the intervening coastal villages were already long-established as trading ports. Later, they also participated in this industry. By the turn of the twentieth century, about 1,200 Arab pearling boats called dhows, were based on the coast of the UAE.

PERSIANS.

Persia is famous for silks, carpets, leather, and gold and silver lace; —the finest pearls are also brought from Persia. They are a fine race of men, & the women are very beautiful. In their dress the Persians keep their heads very warm, always wearing a cap made of lamb-skin; they wear an encumbrance of garments, & prefer scarlet or crimson to any other colour

The text in this eighteenth-century Dutch print describes pearls from the Middle East.

powers, coincided with two important tribal confederations: the Qawasim and the Bani Yas. These local tribes brought power and profits to the region. They are the ancestors of the ruling houses of four of the seven present-day emirates.

Qawasim tribes were a strong presence in the coastal region of the northern emirates. As a tremendous maritime power, the Qawasim helped to establish Sharjah and Ras al-Khaimah as dominant early emirates. At various times during the late seventeenth and early eighteenth centuries, Qawasim influence extended to the Persian side of the gulf.

The Bani Yas, on the other hand, were Bedouin tribes of the interior. The Bani Yas established a base at the Liwa Oasis in southern UAE at the edge of desert known as the the Empty Quarter. This is located near the present-day Saudi border. They would move their capital north to Abu Dhabi Island in 1793. Today, as was the case in the early nineteenth century, Bani Yas tribes rule Abu Dhabi and Dubai.

Bani Yas members engaged in traditional Bedouin activities such as camel herding, small-scale agriculture, and tribal raiding. The raiding led to the extortion of protection money from caravans passing

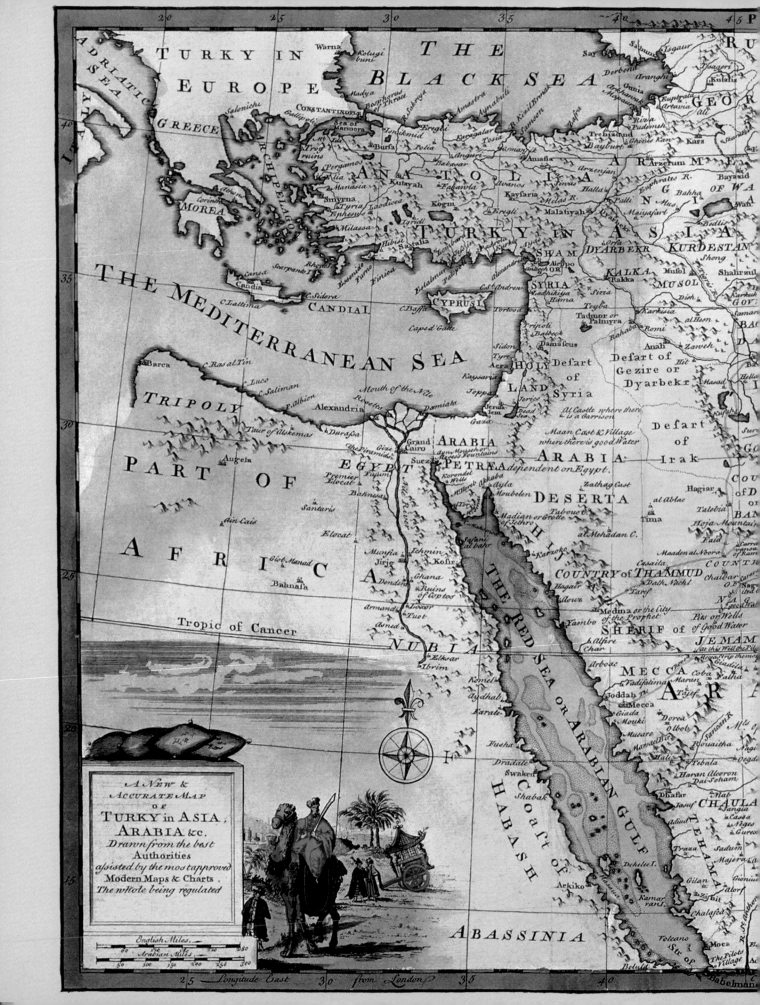

A New &
ACCURATE MAP
OF
TURKY in ASIA,
ARABIA &c.
Drawn from the best
Authorities
assisted by the most approved
Modern Maps & Charts.
The whole being regulated

The Ottoman Empire, as depicted in this seventeenth-century historic map, was experiencing a decline that lasted until the fall of the empire in 1922. The Turks remained powerful until after World War I, when the British governed the land that would later become the United Arab Emirates.

The Persian Gulf

The Persian Gulf is a kidney-shaped body of water in southwestern Asia between Iran and the Arabian Peninsula. Arabs in the region call it the Arabian Gulf. Covering about 100,000 square miles (258,999 sq. km), the gulf is bordered by Iran, Iraq, Kuwait, Saudi Arabia, Bahrain, Qatar, and the United Arab Emirates. The gulf region is home to more than half of the world's reserves of petroleum and natural gas. These resources earn the gulf states billions of dollars each year.

During the 1980s, the Iran-Iraq War saw significant fighting in the gulf. It was also the site of the 1991 Persian Gulf War. During both conflicts, millions of gallons of crude oil were spilled into gulf waters. These acts, along with oil pollution from tanker operations, have adversely affected the gulf environment, perhaps permanently.

This aerial view of the Persian Gulf, the Strait of Hormuz, and the Gulf of Oman was taken from the U.S. space shuttle *Columbia* in 1996. Today's gulf waters are dominated by oil tankers, but smaller trading vessels have sailed the gulf for centuries.

through the Arabian interior. The Bani Yas also took over the slave trade in Arabia when the British outlawed slavery. This decision turned the Buraimi Oasis into eastern Arabia's slave market, a title it retained until the 1950s.

Defining the Enemy

The British paid little attention to the Bani Yas tribes. Similarly, tribal members did not challenge the British maritime position in the gulf. The Qawasim, on the other hand, had a powerful naval presence and control of port cities. By 1800, the Qawasim had a fleet of more than 60 ships and some 20,000 sailors, and they were making trade through the gulf more difficult for the British.

Also competing for a presence in gulf trade activities was the Al-Bu Said family of Oman. The Al-Bu

Saids, however, signed an agreement with the British in 1798. This decision allowed unobstructed trade through the region. In the eyes of the British, the Qawasim were now the primary obstacle to their ongoing success in the gulf. The Al-Bu Saids were the chief rivals of the

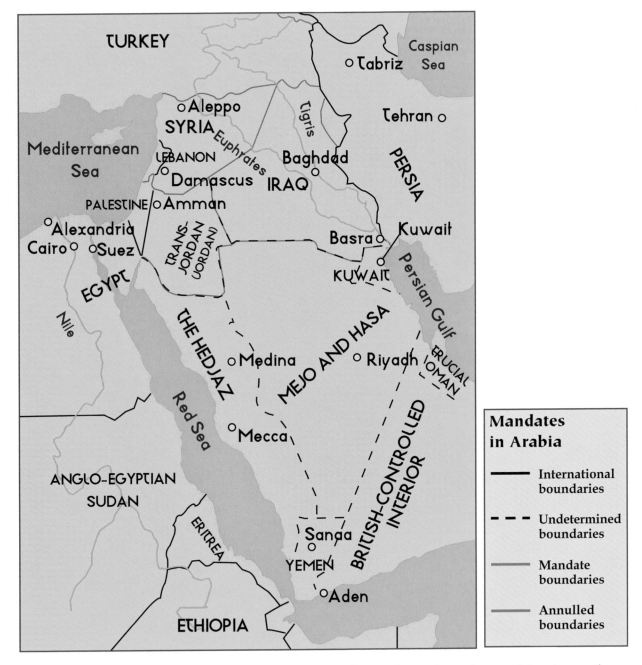

This map shows areas in Arabia that were under British influence during the early part of the nineteenth century. In many cases, these territories are referred to as mandates since they are under the mandate, or authority of, a foreign power. After years of fighting, the powerful British defeated the Qawasim in 1819 and asserted their grip over Oman and the United Arab Emirates. Oman, referred to in this map as Trucial Oman, was given this name by Great Britain after a series of treaties between the two nations.

Qawasim in Arabia. When news of the Omani-British treaty reached Qawasim leaders, it became clear that they now had a new enemy. The Qawasim believed anyone who was an ally of a rival was also a rival. British ships were now fair game for Qawasim military attacks and rebel raids.

The Pirate Coast

For nearly twenty years, Qawasim forces randomly attacked British trading vessels. To this day it is greatly debated who was at fault during these conflicts. Arab historians argue that the British were the outsiders and the Qawasim were merely protecting their livelihood. The British, however, considered these attacks nothing more than piracy and called the lower gulf the Pirate Coast.

By 1819, the British had had enough. They launched a major naval attack from Bombay and cap-

tured or destroyed every Qawasim boat they could find. The following year, the British forced a general treaty of peace on all of the sheikhdoms. Supplemental treaties were issued in 1835 and again in 1853. These agreements were aimed at creating and preserving peace in the region that was then known as the Trucial Coast. It wasn't until 1892, however, that the British would secure control through an exclusive agreement.

The 1892 treaty provided British protection for the emirates from outsiders. This agreement remained in place as long as ruling sheikhs agreed to have no dealings with any foreign power other than Great Britain. With this treaty, the British relationship in the emirates that began in the 1600s was secured for another eighty years. By the time the UAE achieved independence in 1971, the British had dominated the region for more than 150 years.

THE BRITISH AND THE TRUCIAL COAST

In the early 1800s, the area of the United Arab Emirates came to be called the Trucial Coast. This name change was declared in response to the numerous truces and treaties signed between the British and the sheikhdoms of the UAE. From the British point of view, the purpose of these agreements was to keep other foreign forces—namely the French and Russians—out of the Persian Gulf. The British offer of protection to the emirates was simply a means of preserving the profitability of Britain's empire in India. Once these treaties were in place, the British focused on the business of monitoring and promoting trade throughout the gulf, paying little attention to the domestic developments within the emirates.

The results of British domination in the area were the establishment of peace, the introduction of territorial states, and the development of the Trucial States Council in 1952. This body was established to promote cooperation among the seven emirate rulers. The Trucial States Council was the predecessor of the current UAE Supreme Council.

The Inter-Emirate Struggle for Power

At the beginning of the UAE's trucial period, the emirate of Sharjah was its most powerful leader. Staying true to the 1892 treaty, however, Great Britain did not

Foreign trading in the Middle East was booming in the nineteenth century, thanks in part to the opening of Egypt's Suez Canal in 1869, through which this British steamer is traveling. The Suez Canal made sea trade between England and India much faster and more efficient, nearly cutting sailing time in half between London and Bombay. What had been a 12,400-mile (19,950 km) journey around Africa was now shortened to a 7,250-mile (11,670 km) trip that entirely bypassed the continent.

support Sharjah's Qawasim leadership. By the 1900s, power in Sharjah began to shift. Led by a forceful and charismatic Bani Yas sheikh named Zayed Bin Mohammed (Zayed the Great), Abu Dhabi replaced Sharjah as the central power of the emirates. Abu Dhabi retained this position until Mohammed's death in 1909. Although no longer the seat of power, Sharjah did retain its position as the area's main trading center.

Mohammed's death put Abu Dhabi into a state of decline. Mohammed's family fought incessantly over succession rights. With Abu Dhabi's internal struggles in full swing and Sharjah's leadership too weak to dominate, the opportunity for a different emirate to assume authority was presented. Dubai recognized this opportunity and focused its efforts on it.

Aided by a group of Persian traders who left Sharjah over taxation issues, Dubai became the main port of call in the lower gulf for British trade with India. This new position marked the beginning of the emirate's growth as a commercial center.

Led by the Sheikh Rashid bin Saeed al-Maktoum, another descendant of Bani Yas tribes, prosperity followed. Sheikh Saeed, leader of Dubai until his death in 1958, is often referred to as the father of Dubai. Saeed earned this title out of respect for the positive impact he had on his sheikhdom. Sheikh Saeed's son came to power after his death. Sheikh Rashid, who ruled over Dubai from 1958 until 1990, continued to improve Dubai's political and economic position. Using skills he learned while serving as a regent (a substitute ruler) for his father, he turned Dubai into the most important trading center in the gulf.

From Protector to Partner

Change was happening swiftly for Sharjah, Abu Dhabi, and Dubai in the early 1900s. For the British, however, things were very much the same. Although still active in the region, Britain remained more concerned with activities outside the boundaries of the seven emirates. It wasn't until 1932 that any permanent British facility was even constructed within UAE territory. At that time, a rest house was built in Sharjah for the passengers and crew of Britain's former Imperial Airways, currently known as British Airways.

In 1949, however, this lack of involvement would change. For the first time, British forces turned their focus inland to the activities of Abdul Aziz bin Abdul Rahman Al-Saud, the future king of Saudi Arabia. He was making advances with the purpose of conquering the Trucial Coast. Great Britain succeeded in preventing Al-Saud's conquest, chiefly to protect its own empire. Great Britain had no interest in the politics of Saudi Arabia or in the preservation of the emirates.

This involvement with land activities within the UAE was just the beginning for the British. In the years immediately preceding and following World War II (1939–1945)

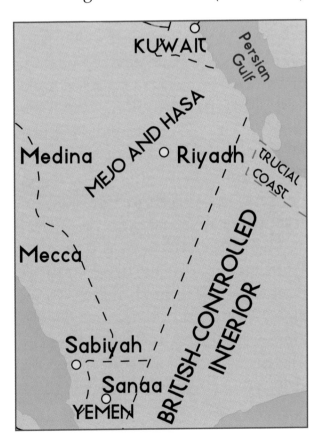

Several peace treaties between Great Britain and various tribal leaders gave rise to eastern Arabia being known as the Trucial Coast during the nineteenth century. As a result of these agreements, separate sheikhdoms, then known as Trucial States, could not form alliances with any foreign nation other than Great Britain.

British involvement in the political, geographic, and economic issues between the emirates increased.

The Quest for Oil

While Dubai was growing, the situation in Abu Dhabi was stabilizing. A new ruler, Sheikh Shakhbut of the al-Nahyan family, had come to power in Abu Dhabi in 1928. It was a difficult time for the new ruler. The political structure of Abu Dhabi was unstable, and the economy had suffered tremendously because the pearling industry had collapsed. Sheikh Shakhbut wanted to end the conditions of poverty for his people. Out of his desperation for a solution was born an idea that would eventually save the UAE and other Persian Gulf countries. It would also change the way the British ran their affairs in the Trucial Coast.

Sheikh Shakhbut wanted to allow British companies the opportunity to drill for oil. To do so he needed to sign what are known as oil concessions with the excavating companies. Oil concessions are agreements to drill within the UAE in exchange for a percentage of the resulting profits. Concessions could not be granted to the emirates, however, without the establishment of specific inter-emirate borders. Eager to secure the largest possible piece of the pie, all seven local rulers claimed enormous parcels of land. Each ruler was unwilling to give up any territory to their neighbors. Eventually, the British government abandoned its policy of staying out of internal affairs and drew these boundaries on its own.

The resulting borders were formalized but never wholeheartedly agreed upon. Ambiguities resulting from these border decisions remained the subject of inter-emirate debate. By 1939, the British-defined boundaries were in place. Sheikh Shakhbut became the first emirate ruler to allow a British company to drill for oil. It would take nearly thirty years, however, before petroleum would be exported from the region. The three decades that followed remained politically and economically challenging for the UAE.

5 THE OIL ERA

Although Abu Dhabi is currently the wealthiest member of the United Arab Emirates, the two decades following the death of Zayed Bin Mohammed marked a period of instability in its history. Although Sheikh Shakhbut was able to establish control in Abu Dhabi, the sheikhdom was virtually impoverished as a result of the failed pearling industry.

Shakhbut, however, knew the situation for all of the emirates was temporary. Following his initiative of the early 1930s, the rulers of the seven sheikhdoms began signing oil concession agreements with the British-owned Iraq Petroleum Company (IPC). Discovering oil in the UAE was seen as the total solution to the weak economies of the emirates. Unfortunately, it would take another twenty years of poverty before the emirates received any oil revenues. In the meantime, territorial controversies preoccupied emirate leaders.

Controversial Claims

Oil was positively discovered in Abu Dhabi in 1949. At that time, leaders from Saudi Arabia asserted that the Buraimi Oasis on the border with Oman was theirs by a historical claim. This claim was made based on the assumption by the Saudi government that the land had once been a part of the first Saudi

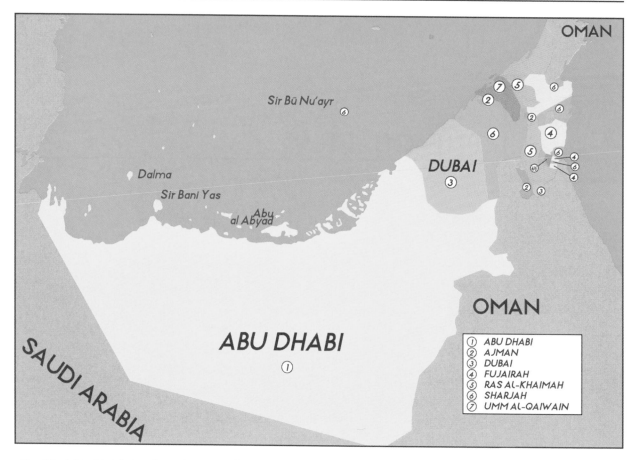

Abu Dhabi is highlighted on this map that shows its relationship to Oman and the other six emirates of the UAE. Petroleum was discovered in Abu Dhabi in 1949, a development that sparked interest in the region from neighboring Saudi Arabia. Shortly after the discovery of petroleum was confirmed in Abu Dhabi, Saudi leaders claimed a historical right to its territory.

Empire. In reality, the Saudi claim was provoked by the prospect of oil deposits beneath the fertile oasis. In order to lay claim to what would soon be a tremendous moneymaker for the region, Saudi officials completely disregarded the 100-plus years the land had spent divided between Abu Dhabi and Oman.

Geologists associated with Aramco, the Saudi oil concessionaire in Saudi Arabia, had reported to the Saudi government their suspicion of expansive oil reserves under the oasis. Just as was the case between the emirates, the border with Saudi Arabia was also largely undefined and often disputed. Saudi officials tried to capitalize on this fact with their 1949 claim. The Saudi government wanted to control an even greater percentage of the total oil supply in the Persian Gulf.

Although it would take nearly thirty years to reach a conclusion, the Saudi claim was neither disproved nor substantiated. In 1966, all Saudi forces that had moved into the area fled, and the border through the Buraimi Oasis was formalized. Saudi Arabia dropped its claim entirely in 1974 under the stipulation that Abu Dhabi compensate the Saudis with a percentage of the oil revenues it received from the oasis reserves.

From Possibilities to Profits

Nearly ten years passed before the IPC's oil explorations in the UAE made significant process. With his sheikhdom still in poverty's grasp, Sheikh Shakhbut was desperate for the oil discovery that would change the lives of the 15,000 who lived in Abu Dhabi. In 1953, he signed another concession to an Anglo-French consortium, this time for offshore drilling. Five years later, these prospectors made the first oil strike on the Trucial Coast, in the waters off Abu Dhabi's mainland. Not long after this discovery, it became apparent that Abu Dhabi's reserves were enormous. The exporting of oil from Abu Dhabi began in 1962. Soon Sheikh Shakhbut realized that his emirate would become a wealthy state.

Now a rich man, the sheikh became distrustful of banks and sus-picious of the foreign oil companies that brought this newfound wealth to his homeland. Eventually, British officials worked with the al-Nahyan family to orchestrate Shakhbut's removal, or deposition. The longtime governor of Al-Ain, Zayed Shakhbut, who was also Sheikh Shakhbut's brother, became the new sheikh of Abu Dhabi in 1966. Zayed had had an excellent record of fair leadership in Al-Ain,

Jacques Y. Cousteau, seen here in a shark-proof cage, is being lowered into the Persian Gulf. The famous underwater explorer was commissioned by BP Exploration Company, the prospecting subsidiary of the British Petroleum Company, to investigate the waters off Abu Dhabi in the Persian Gulf. In this area, BP held a concession over 12,000 square miles (31,080 sq. km) for a period of sixty-five years.

and he moved quickly to use the emirate's new wealth. He transformed Abu Dhabi into a progressive, modern society. He also shared the new wealth with the less fortunate emirates not blessed with oil reserves of their own.

Today, the UAE's proven hydrocarbon reserves amount to about 98 billion barrels of oil—enough to last well into the twenty-second century at present extraction and usage rates. These reserves represent 10 percent of the world's total oil resources, the third largest after Saudi Arabia and Iraq. The majority of these reserves are found within the emirate of Abu Dhabi. Dubai, Sharjah, and Ras al-Khaimah have hydrocarbon reserves, although they are minimal by comparison.

Natural gas discoveries, also located primarily within the emirate of Abu Dhabi, are estimated to be enough to supply the world for at least another 350 years. These resources have positioned the UAE as the fourth largest producer of natural gas after Russia, Iran, and Qatar. As of yet, none of the remaining six emirates have made significant discoveries of oil or gas deposits. Were it not for its responsibility to these emirates, Abu Dhabi's 2.5 million residents would boast the highest per capita income in the world.

Separate and Not Equal

Oil revenues firmly established Abu Dhabi as the economic and political leader among the emirates. The adjacent sheikhdom, Dubai, continued its efforts to remain the region's trading center despite discovering its own cache of oil and gas deposits. Sharjah, the onetime powerful emirate, had let its primary port be divided. As a result, the sheikhdom's economy entered an unrecoverable decline. Unfortunately, oil and gas discoveries there would not be enough to return Sharjah to its former position of power, leaving it a "poor cousin" to its wealthier neighbors. Over time, the other emirates developed economies based on agriculture, fishing, and, to a lesser degree, tourism.

The Road to Independence

Change was happening quickly throughout the entire Middle East in the 1950s and 1960s. In addition to the economic boom beginning in the UAE, pan-Arabism—a movement for greater cooperation among Arab or Islamic nations—was flourishing. Cooperation, however, was not the central theme of these changes.

A coup in Egypt in 1954 would bring a young leader named Gamal Abdel Nasser to power. Two years

OPEC and the Oil Crisis

The Organization of Petroleum Exporting Countries (OPEC) is an association of nations that rely on oil exports for their income. Since 1960, its member countries have worked together to increase revenues from the sale of oil on the world market.

Oil production exceeded world demand before OPEC was formed. This surplus prompted several American and European oil companies to reduce concessions to host countries by cutting the posted price of crude oil. The price cuts adversely affected the economies of many oil-producing nations. The OPEC organization was founded in response to these losses.

Initially, OPEC had little influence on international oil prices. The 1970s, however, saw a worldwide increase in the need for oil that outpaced the production capabilities of non-OPEC countries. In addition, armed Arab-Israeli conflicts occurring throughout the Middle East in the 1970s caused many of the oil-rich Arab countries to cease production and exportation to countries that supported Israel. In response, OPEC raised prices significantly.

By the 1980s, production was again able to satisfy demand, and prices were cut. OPEC also implemented a quota system designed to help petroleum prices remain stable. But for a brief increase that resulted from the 1991 Gulf War, petroleum prices have done just that.

Today, OPEC members produce about 40 percent of the world's oil and control about 75 percent of the available recoverable reserves. In addition to the United Arab Emirates, OPEC member nations include Algeria, Indonesia, Iran, Iraq, Kuwait, Libya, Nigeria, Qatar, Saudi Arabia, Venezuela (not shown), and Gabon.

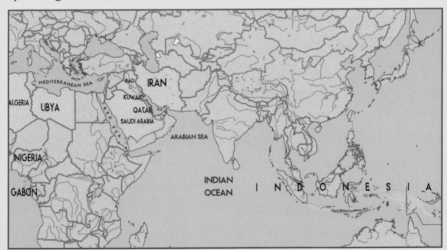

Member countries of OPEC are shown in this map. Inspired by the nationalistic attitudes of the 1950s, many poverty-stricken but petroleum-rich nations sought to control the price of oil on the world market. This was especially true in 1969, when the price of oil had fallen to $1.40 per barrel. In 1973, when Arab nations imposed an oil embargo on the nations that supported Israel, such as the United States, the price of oil increased by 130 percent. When the price dropped again in 1990, OPEC members worked together to cut back on oil production in order to increase world demand.

OPEC representatives of each member country meet in Abu Dhabi in 1978 to discuss the production, demand, and price of crude oil. The late 1970s saw a rise in the world's production of petroleum, so OPEC representatives met frequently to stabilize the demand for crude oil by controlling its production and price.

later he incited a crisis in Suez, a city and port in northeastern Egypt. Although not directly involved in the Suez Crisis, the chain of events that followed in the Middle East set the stage within the seven sheikhdoms for massive changes.

With their political and military attention focused on events in the Suez, the British allowed greater local participation in the governments of their protectorate states. In 1968, they made the startling announcement that all of their defense agreements east of Suez would be terminated. The British estimated that their complete withdrawal from the region would occur by 1971.

6 INDEPENDENCE AND INTERNATIONAL ACCEPTANCE

The 1970s began a period of unprecedented growth and prosperity for the emirates. Not long after the British announcement to leave the gulf, the rulers of Abu Dhabi and Dubai announced that they would form a federation. Initially, the Federation of Arab Emirates included the whole of the Trucial Coast as well as Qatar and Bahrain. These nine emirates were unified in their desire for security, but they also faced obstacles. Mostly these problems were related to the region's internal boundary disputes.

A Federation Forms

Prior to their departure, the British worked with the leaders of the emirates to establish guidelines for their unification. In June 1971, just six months before British withdrawal, Bahrain decided it was secure enough on its own. Six of the sheikhdoms had reached an agreement on a federal constitution in July of that same year. Bahrain, on the other hand, announced in August that it would not join the federation. Qatar followed suit less than three weeks later. On the eve of British withdrawal, two obstacles remained a threat to the formation of the United Arab Emirates.

First, Ras al-Khaimah had not agreed to the constitution drafted in July. Its ruler, Sheikh Saqr bin Mohammed al Qasimi, was holding out, hoping that

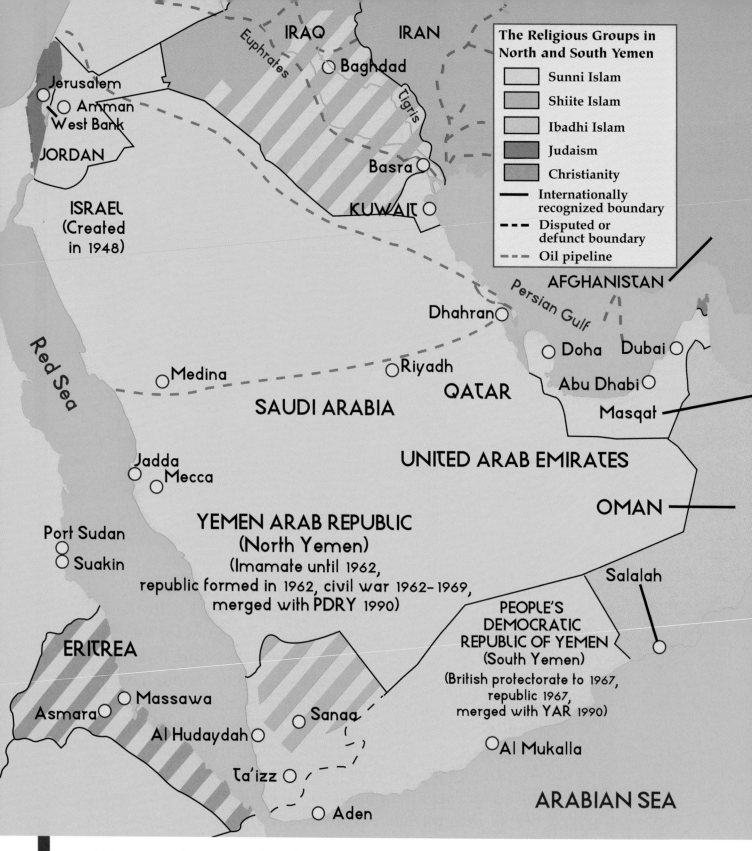

The Religious Groups in North and South Yemen

- ☐ Sunni Islam
- ☐ Shiite Islam
- ☐ Ibadhi Islam
- ■ Judaism
- ■ Christianity
- ── Internationally recognized boundary
- ─ ─ Disputed or defunct boundary
- ─ ─ Oil pipeline

IRAQ

IRAN

Baghdad

Euphrates

Tigris

Jerusalem

Amman

West Bank

JORDAN

ISRAEL
(Created
in 1948)

Basra

KUWAIT

AFGHANISTAN

Persian Gulf

Dhahran

Doha

Dubai

Red Sea

Medina

Riyadh

QATAR

Abu Dhabi

Masqat

SAUDI ARABIA

UNITED ARAB EMIRATES

Jadda

Mecca

OMAN

YEMEN ARAB REPUBLIC
(North Yemen)
(Imamate until 1962,
republic formed in 1962, civil war 1962–1969,
merged with PDRY 1990)

Port Sudan

Suakin

Salalah

PEOPLE'S
DEMOCRATIC
REPUBLIC OF YEMEN
(South Yemen)

ERITREA

(British protectorate to 1967,
republic 1967,
merged with YAR 1990)

Massawa

Asmara

Sanaa

Al Hudaydah

Al Mukalla

Ta'izz

ARABIAN SEA

Aden

This is a map of Eritrea, Israel, Saudi Arabia, Jordan, Kuwait, Oman, North and South Yemen, the United Arab Emirates, Qatar, and southern Iraq and Iran after 1945. Besides illustrating recognized and disputed boundaries, the map shows the general concentration of religions throughout the region. Many Arab countries on the Arabian Peninsula changed dramatically during the twentieth century as they emerged as independent nations no longer under the control of Great Britain and France.

oil deposits would be discovered in his sheikhdom to support independence. It would take another two months before Sheikh Saqr agreed to join the federation.

The second obstacle was Iran's occupation of the islands of Abu Musa and the Greater and Lesser Tunbs. All three islands had been claimed by the UAE, specifically by Sharjah and Ras al-Khaimah. Despite the lack of resolve regarding the ownership of these islands, the United Arab Emirates was formally recognized as a united nation on December 2, 1971. At the time, few foreign critics believed that the federation could succeed.

Sheikh Zayed bin Sultan al-Nahyan of Abu Dhabi became president of the UAE. The ruler of Dubai, Sheikh Rashid bin Saeed al-Maktoum, acted as vice president and prime minister. Under their joint

The sheikhs of the seven Arab emirates are seen in this photograph around the time of UAE independence in 1971. The emirates are governed by the Supreme Council of Rulers, which is composed of a hereditary line of leaders. The Supreme Council elects one president and vice president, each for a five-year term, and the president appoints a prime minister and a cabinet of forty members chosen by each emirate. There are no political parties in the emirates.

Sheikh Zayed bin Sultan al-Nahyan of Abu Dhabi, who became president of the UAE at the time of its independence from Great Britain in 1971, was photographed after taking part in the Arab Summit of 1987. Sheik Zayed has since been reelected every five years by the UAE's Supreme Council members, but his health is deteriorating. Sheikh Zayed will be succeeded by his son, Sheikh Khalifah, at the time of his death.

leadership, the UAE has become a model of Arab unity.

A Time of Stability

Since its independence, the UAE has been one of the most stable countries in the Arab world. This does not mean, however, that it has not experienced controversy. Border disputes among the emirates continued throughout the 1970s and 1980s. In 1976, Sheikh Zayed threatened to resign as president if the other six emirs did not settle their outstanding disputes. Within three years, an agreement was reached that created a stronger federation.

Each emir maintained control over his emirate's internal activities, though it was clear that certain systems required an overarching federal structure. In response to this need, Zayed established unified welfare and legal systems, a police force, and telecommunications networks. Today the emirates are known as much for their infrastructure and policies on

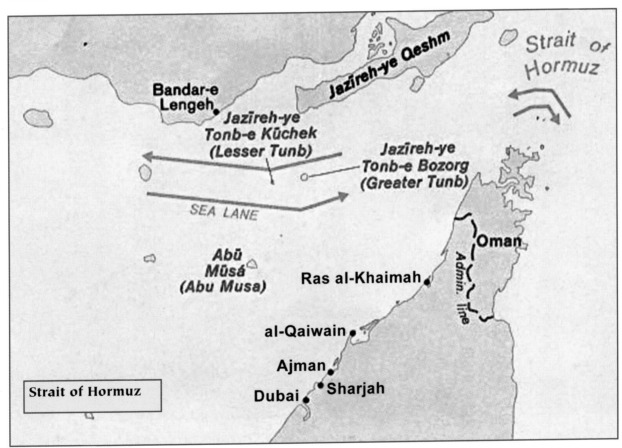

Common areas of travel through the Persian Gulf to the Strait of Hormuz and the Gulf of Oman can be seen in this CIA map of the waterways surrounding the UAE and southern Iran. The Greater and Lesser Tunb Islands, which are currently occupied by Iran, are also visible. These waters have been used as shipping lanes for thousands of years.

social and economic reform as they are for their wealth.

At the same time, regional instability has presented a threat to the future of the emirates. Intermittent Arab-Israeli wars, Islamic revolutions in Iran, the Iran-Iraq War, and the unresolved issue surrounding Iran's invasion of Abu Musa and the Tunbs have all threatened the UAE. But the country survived and prospered largely due to the prowess of its president. Zayed used the oil wealth of Abu Dhabi to benefit all of the emirates.

Perhaps one of the most ingenious actions in Zayed's preservation of the emirates was the formation of the Arabian Gulf Cooperation Council (AGCC). With Iran and Iraq busily fighting each other, the six oil-rich gulf nations (Saudi Arabia, Kuwait, Bahrain, Qatar, Oman, and the UAE) seized the opportunity to establish an organization of their own. Modeled

Representatives from six Arab countries are members of the Arabian Gulf Cooperation Council (AGCC). Standing from left to right are Saudi prince Sultan ibn Abdelaziz; Kuwait's deputy prime minister, Sheikh Sabah Al-Ahmed Al-Jaber Al-Sabah; the emir of Qatar, Sheikh Hamad bin Khalifa Al-Thani; the deputy prime minister of Oman, Sayyid Fahd bin Mahmud Al Said; Saudi crown prince Abdullah; King Hamad bin Isa Al Khalifa of Bahrain; and the president of the United Arab Emirates, Sheikh Zayed bin Sultan al-Nahyan.

after the European Economic Community (EEC), the AGCC was formed in 1981. Ultimately not as powerful a union as its members had hoped, the AGCC intended to promote solidarity and economic, political, and social cooperation among the oil-producing nations of the Arabian Peninsula.

A Good International Neighbor

The UAE quickly earned the respect of the international community. Under Zayed's leadership, the country became an outspoken supporter of the Middle East peace process and a loyal ally to the United States.

The UAE was one of the first countries to offer support to Kuwait after the Iraqi invasion of the country in 1990. It also offered support to United Nations forces that restored peace to the war-weary country of Somalia. And in response to Serbian genocidal attacks on Bosnia's Muslim community, Zayed made impassioned pleas for international intervention. In addition, the UAE has been one of the most financially generous in the world. Since its independence, it has allocated more than $5 billion in aid to more than forty developing countries.

The strategic location of the UAE and its rich oil and gas reserves also require the maintenance of a military force. After the Persian Gulf War, Zayed began a defense spending program equal to between 4 and 6 percent of the country's annual income. At the turn of the century, the UAE boasted a massive military with more than 65,000 members, including women.

Internal Scandal

The UAE's involvement in the 1990–1991 Persian Gulf War earned the country tremendous international support and strengthened its relations with the United States. Those same relationships were challenged in the summer of 1991. At that time, the emirates received unflattering attention in the form of financial scandal.

Western bank regulators led by the Bank of England shut down the Bank of Credit and Commerce International (BCCI), of which Abu Dhabi was the major shareholder. This collapse posed a delicate political problem for Abu Dhabi. It balanced negotiations regarding the BCCI's future with the need to protect the bank's local customers. Abu Dhabi responded by buying all BCCI branches throughout the emirates and reconstituting them as the Union National Bank.

7 THE MODERN UAE

DOHA
○ Al Wakrah

QATAR

Dalma

Sir Bani Yas

Jabal Dhanna ━━━

Ar Ruways ━━

SAUDI ARABIA

Of the seven emirates, Abu Dhabi and Dubai are the most well known. The other five also play important roles in defining the United Arab Emirates. Distinct in economic offerings, the emirates do have two things in common. Each of the seven main cities shares its name with the emirate itself, and each lies on the coast of the Persian Gulf.

Abu Dhabi, also the capital of the country, is centered on an island; Dubai, Sharjah, and Ras al-Khaimah are on creeks that extend inland from the gulf; and Ajman, Umm al-Qaiwain, and Fujairah are on sand spits that each curl around a lagoon. A sand spit is a low, sandy area jutting out into a lake or sea.

Abu Dhabi

Literally translated, "Abu Dhabi" means "Father of the Gazelle." The largest of the

This map illustrates the present-day boundaries of the seven emirates and their position on the gulf coast. The new wealth brought into the country after the discovery of petroleum has raised the standard of living for most UAE residents. Now with a sizable surplus thanks to foreign trade, the UAE has been transformed into a modern state with an improved infrastructure and public services. However, crude oil exports are expected to run out within a century, so the government is working to increase private business enterprises in order to create new jobs.

Strait of
Hormuz

PERSIAN GULF

Tunb
claimed by Iran
and U.A.E
Abu Musa

OMAN

Ar Rams
Ras al-Khaimah
Hamriyyah
Khatt
Diqdaqah

Umm al-Qaiwain

Badiyah

Ajman
Sharjah
Dubai
Adh Dhayd
Khawr Fakkan
Fujairah

Al Haba

ABU DHABI

Abu
al Abyad

Al Maqta

Tarif

Al `Ayn

Ghayathi

OMAN

Al Mariyah

'Aradah

(unofficial border)

seven emirates and home to the country's capital city of the same name, Abu Dhabi takes its name from legend. According to the story, a party of hunters followed a gazelle from the Liwa Oasis to a collection of coastal islands in the gulf. When they arrived, they found a freshwater spring, and the gazelles stopped to drink. The hunters began a settlement there in 1790, and one year later the emirate was founded.

Dubai

Traveling eastward from Abu Dhabi, Dubai is the second largest and second wealthiest of the seven emirates. It is also the commercial center of the Middle East. Known for centuries to traders of spices, gold, slaves, and sandalwood, sailing vessels known as dhows have moored in Dubai since its founding in the early 1800s.

Archaeological discoveries in the areas of Jumeirah and Mina Siyahi

This fruit and vegetable market in Abu Dhabi (left) is a popular place to purchase foods for daily meals. Most residents of the emirates buy their foods in open-air marketplaces like this one, which are known as souks. The Grand Mosque in Dubai (right) is the city's tallest minaret, the place from which Muslims are called to pray. Although the structure appears to be old, it is actually a new mosque built to look like the original structure that was erected in 1900.

also indicate that the region was an important stop for overland trade via caravans between Mesopotamia and Oman. Today, these once remote areas are linked by four-lane highways and boast magnificent residential suburbs.

Sharjah

Once a central port in Middle East shipping, Sharjah lies in the shadow of its southwestern neighbor, Dubai. Located in the third largest emirate, the city of Sharjah is the oldest of the country's three main cities. Dating back to at least 1490, ancient maps also refer to the city as Quiximi and Scharge.

Already a shipping power by the time British interests in the region boomed, Sharjah's progress slowed by the 1940s when its port city silted up and its shipping routes were diverted to Dubai. Today, Sharjah contains the main administrative centers for the

These tuna fishermen rest on a dhow between excursions in Sharjah. A dhow is a simple Arab boat made out of wood. Dhows have been used in the Persian Gulf for hundreds of years. They are usually used for trading, pearl diving, and general transportation. Tourists are commonly seen aboard smaller Arab boats called *abras*, used to navigate near the shoreline of the gulf.

whole of the emirates and is noted for its public parks and elegant mosques.

Ajman

The smallest of the seven emirates, Ajman is little more than the city itself. A combination of beautiful beaches, inland enclaves, and fertile mountain villages, Ajman is known for its shipbuilding. From as early as the third millennium BC, pearling dhows sailed from its shores and are still built on its sheltered creek.

Unfortunately Ajman hasn't experienced the boom enjoyed by the other emirates as a result of their gas and oil discoveries. It has instead found a way to reap some financial benefits by updating its boat-building traditions. Today Ajman's main port houses one of the UAE's largest ship repair companies responsible for oil field supply boats.

The wooden hulls of Arab dhows stand in a boat-building yard in the small coastal emirate of Ajman, which faces the Persian Gulf. Ajman has long been the home of Arab pearl divers. Ajman also houses a historical fort at its center, as well as the agricultural village of Masfat.

Umm al-Qaiwain

Umm al-Qaiwain ("Mother of the Powers" in Arabic) is the second smallest emirate in area. It is also the least populated, with only 40,000 inhabitants. Umm al-Qaiwain includes the island of As Siniyyah, a wildlife haven that is home to herons, cormorants, turtles, sea snakes, and the ancient dugong (sea cow). Archaeological excavations there reveal that its inhabitants were hunting dugong some 5,000 years ago.

This 1995 postage stamp is from Umm al-Qaiwain. Umm al-Qaiwain is a small emirate located just north of Ajman. Its 35,000 residents are mainly fishermen and date farmers.

Ras al-Khaimah

Ras al-Khaimah is the northernmost emirate on the west coast. Divided by the Hajar Mountains, Ras al-Khaimah boasts a separate enclave in the heart of the mountains and a number of islands. These include the long-disputed islands of Greater and Lesser Tunb, occupied by Iran since 1971.

An early maritime power in the gulf, Ras al-Khaimah was a base of the Qawasim "pirates" in the nineteenth century. Conflicts with the British led it to being known as the Pirate Coast. During this time activities centered in the ancient city of Julfar. Once thought to have been a mythical place, archaeologists and historians now know that Julfar was an ancient and flourishing port city.

The Hajar Mountains are located along the western coast of the United Arab Emirates. The mountains reach their highest point of about 6,562 feet (2,000 meters) in Musandam, an area known as Ru'us Al-Jibal, or the "Heads of the Mountains."

Fujairah

With the exception of some isolated areas belonging to Sharjah, Fujairah is the only emirate situated on the Gulf of Oman. Framed by the Hajar Mountains and blessed with dramatic scenery, Fujairah is poised to continue building an economy based on tourism. The port of Fujairah is also one of the world's top oil bunkering ports.

Fujairah is home to the historic city of Dibba. In antiquity, Fujairah's remote location kept it safe from foreign and tribal influences. As a result, the culture within Fujairah is uniquely Arab.

Prosperity in Diversity

Since the early 1990s, the United Arab Emirates has maintained its status as a world business center. The country has been a key player among

This is an aerial view of Fujairah, the youngest of the seven emirates. Fujairah rests on the Gulf of Oman, and residents claim that its beaches make it one of the UAE's most attractive regions. Tourists also flock to Fujairah for its wealth of archaeological sites.

Arab nations and has won admiration for its diplomacy. Always focused on creating unity among all the Arab nations, the UAE is an active member of the Arab League and the United Nations.

No longer isolated, the UAE is a multinational, multicultural center of world business. Its population, although predominantly Arab, is diverse, with only about 20 to 25 percent of its citizens being Emiratis, or nationals.

The majority of people living in the emirates are expatriates, a word used to describe foreign residents. The UAE's expatriate population is largely from India, Pakistan, Iran, and Southeast Asia, yet the United States and several European countries also have a solid expatriate population there, stemming primarily from the oil boom of the 1960s and 1970s. Although the government has recently introduced programs aimed at "re-emiratizing" the emirates, the large foreign population is a welcome part of its society.

Outsiders are not simply drawn to the emirates for the high standard of living and tax-free shopping. There

The UAE is brimming over with modern skyscrapers and unique architecture such as the Volcano Fountain of Abu Dhabi, which was built in 2000. Because of a rise in the price of crude oil, the emirates have seen an influx of elaborate construction throughout the country, most notably in its eclectic public structures and corporate buildings.

are also superior public services, excellent education and health-care systems, and little crime.

Without a doubt, the UAE is one of the twentieth century's success stories, witnessing the most unique social and economic reversals in world history. Less than fifty years ago, the UAE could offer little in terms of prosperity to its citizens. Today they enjoy the privileges of a first-class world economy that is steadily growing. In fact, with international interests increasing throughout the emirates, it is likely that the situation in the UAE will only improve.

TIMELINE

5000–3000 BC Archaeological evidence of early inhabitants.

3000 BC The Magan Empire in northern Arabia profits from copper mining.

2500–2000 BC The Umm al-Nar period.

2000 BC Arab tribes arrive from southwest and central Arabia.

1200–300 BC Camels are domesticated. Irrigation systems are developed.

AD 226–640 The Sassanid period; Persian forces control sea trade.

632 Death of the prophet Muhammad; Islam spreads throughout Arabia.

800–900 Arab seafaring and trading reach their zenith.

1498 Portuguese explorers enter the Persian Gulf.

1747 The Qawasim of Ras al-Khaimah rise to power.

1761 Abu Dhabi is founded.

1820 The General Treaty of Peace and British Involvement in the emirates begins with a British campaign to quash the Qawasim.

1830s Pearl trade is at its height.

1892 The Exclusive Agreement is signed.

1930s Abu Dhabi and Dubai emerge as leader states in the region.

1936–1952 Leaders of the Trucial Coast sign oil concessions with the Iraq Petroleum Company; exploration begins.

1949 Oil is discovered in Abu Dhabi.

1952 The formation of the Trucial States Council.

1960 OPEC is founded.

1962 Oil exporting begins in the emirates.

1966 Oil is discovered in Dubai.

1968 Great Britain declares its intention to withdraw from the gulf by 1971.

1971 The United Arab Emirates is formally inaugurated on December 2 with six member states: Abu Dhabi, Dubai, Sharjah, Ajman, Umm al-Qaiwain, and Fujairah.

1972 Ras al-Khaimah becomes the seventh emirate to join the UAE.

1973 OPEC quadruples crude oil prices.

1974 Saudi Arabia drops its claim to the Burami Oasis.

1981 The AGCC (Arabian Gulf Cooperation Council) is formed.

1991 The UAE takes part in the Gulf War against Iraq.

2000 The UAE pays $8 billion for U.S.-produced fighter jets and missiles from a U.S. company.

2002 AGCC leaders meet in Muscat to implement a new economic agreement to replace the 1981 agreement to form a unified economic bloc in the Middle East.

2003 UAE switches from conventional to unleaded fuel.

GLOSSARY

aflaj An ancient channel irrigation system developed to bring water via underground systems from the mountains to drier desert regions.

Arab A person born or living in Arabia or another Arabic-speaking country.

Bedouin Nomadic Arab of the Arabian, Syrian, or North African deserts.

caliph A successor of Muhammad as temporal and spiritual head of Islam.

concession An agreement between parties to undertake and profit from a specified activity.

concessionaire A person or a company that is given land by a government concession or who operates a business or sells a product in a specific place.

coup (coup d'état) A French term meaning "blow to the state" that refers to a sudden unexpected overthrow of a government by outsiders.

desert democracy The Arab tribal system of ruling by consultation and consensus.

dhow A ship used along the coasts of Arabia, India, and eastern Africa in sea-based industries.

emir A ruler, chief, or commander in an Islamic country.

emirate The state or jurisdiction of an emir.

Emiratis Citizens or nationals of the countries of the United Arab Emirates.

enclave A distinct territorial, cultural, or social unit enclosed within a foreign territory.

expatriate One who lives and works in a country in which he or she does not have citizenship.

federation A union of organizations.

Islam The Muslim religion, based on the teachings of the prophet Muhammad.

mandate The authority given to an elected group of people, such as a government, to perform an action or govern a country.

oasis A fertile green area in an otherwise barren desert region.

OPEC The Organization of Petroleum Exporting Countries, founded in 1960 with eleven member countries.

sect A religious denomination; a group adhering to a distinctive doctrine or to a leader.

Semite A member of any group of peoples of southwestern Asia, chiefly represented now by the Jews and Arabs but in ancient times also by the Babylonians, Assyrians, Aramaeans, Canaanites, and Phoenicians.

semitic Relating to or characteristic of the Semites.

Shia A sect of Islam that supports the claims of Ali and his line and their presumptive right to the leadership of the Muslim community.

sheikh An Arab chief; the leader of a family or tribe.

sheikhdom The territory ruled by a sheikh.

Sunni A sect of Islam that supports the traditional method of election of the caliphate and accept the Ummayad line of leaders.

trucial Having to do with being bound by a truce or treaty.

wadi A shallow, usually sharply-defined depression in a desert region.

FOR MORE INFORMATION

U.S Embassy of the United
   Arab Emirates
1255 22nd Street NW, Suite 700
Washington, DC 20037
(202) 243-2400

Web Site

Due to the changing nature of Internet links, the Rosen Publishing Group, Inc., has developed an online list of Web sites related to the subject of this book. This site is updated regularly. Please use this link to access the list:

http://www.rosenlinks.com/liha/unae

FOR FURTHER READING

Augustin, Byron. *United Arab Emirates* (Enchantment of the World). New York: Children's Press, 2002.

Crocetti, Gina L. *Culture Shock! United Arab Emirates* (Culture Shock Guides). Portland, OR: Graphic Arts Center Publishing Co., 2002.

Johnson, Julia. *United Arab Emirates* (Major World Nations). Broomall, PA: Chelsea House, 2000.

McCoy, Lisa. *United Arab Emirates* (Modern Middle East Nations). Broomall, PA: Mason Crest, 2003.

BIBLIOGRAPHY

Callan, Lou, and Gordon Robison. *Oman and the United Arab Emirates*, first edition. Victoria, Australia: Lonely Planet Publications, 2000.

Humphreys, Andrew, et. al. *Middle East*, third edition. Victoria, Australia: Lonely Planet Publications, 2000.

Infoplease.com. "Arabia." Retrieved January 12, 2003 (http://www.infoplease.com/ceb/world/AO856661.html).

Infoplease.com. "United Arab Emirates." Retrieved December 26, 2002 (http://www.infoplease.com/ceb/world/AO861702.html).

Landen, Roger Geran. "United Arab Emirates." World Book Online Americas Edition. Retrieved December 26, 2002 (http://www.worldbookonline.com/ar?/na/ar/co/ar575520.html).

Peck, Malcolm C. "United Arab Emirates." Microsoft Encarta Online Encyclopedia 2002. Retrieved January 12, 2003 (http://encarta.msn.com).

Robison, Gordon. *The Gulf States*. Victoria, Australia: Lonely Planet Publications, 1996.

Stannard, Dorothy, and Brian Bell, eds. *Insight Guide: Oman and the UAE*. London: The Discovery Channel/APA Publications, Langenscheidt Publishers, Inc., 1998.

INDEX

About the Author

Amy Romano has a master's degree in business administration from American International College in Springfield, Massachusetts, and has written a number of magazine articles on a range of topics for both consumer and business-to-business publications. Amy is a member of the adjunct faculty at Western International University in Arizona, where she lives with her husband, Don, and their children, Claudia, Sam, and Jack. She has authored several books for young adults.

Photo Credits

Cover (map), pp. 1 (foreground), 4–5, 40, 52–53 © 2002 Geoatlas; cover (background), pp. 1 (background), 26–27, 49 courtesy of the General Libraries, the University of Texas at Austin; cover (top left), p. 28 © The Art Archive/British Library; cover (bottom left), p. 50 © AP/Wide World Photos; cover (bottom right), p. 54 (right) © Alain LeGarsmeur/ Impact Photos; p. 6 © Maps.com; p. 8 © Library of Congress, Geography and Map Division; p. 9 © Gianni Dagli Orti/Corbis; p. 10 (inset) © Erich Lessing/Art Resource; pp. 10, 14–15, 18–19, 20, 22–23, 33, 37, 43, 46–47 maps designed by Tahara Hasan; p. 11, 56, 57 (bottom) © Christine Osborne/Corbis; p. 12 © Peter Sanders; p. 13 © Arne Hordalic/Corbis; pp. 17, 21 © Archivo Iconografico, S.A./Corbis; p. 24 © The Art Archive/National Library Cario/Dagli Orti; p. 29 © Hulton-Deutsch/ Corbis; pp. 30–31 © The Art Archive/Naval Museum Genoa/Dagli Orti; p. 32 © 1996 Corbis; p. 36 © Scheufler Collection/ Corbis; p. 41 © Underwood and Underwood/Corbis; p. 44 © Bettmann/Corbis; p. 47 © Ramesh Shukla/Corbis Sygma; p. 48 © Alain Nogues/Corbis Sygma; p. 54 (left) © Caroline Penn/Impact Photos; p. 55 © K. M. Westermann/Corbis; p. 57 (top) © Corbis Sygma; p. 58 © Francoise de Mulder/Corbis; p. 59 © Jon Hicks/Corbis.

Designer: Tahara Hasan; **Editor:** Joann Jovinelly;
Photo Researcher: Elizabeth Loving